CONTENTS

ANIMAL BABIES

DOS AND DON'TS

DOGGY DATA

DREAM HOME

DOGS, DOGS, DOGS!

Although there's a dizzying number of dog breeds, they are divided into six groups according to their relationship with humans over time. Here they are:

TERRIER

There are lots of different Terrier breeds and they are all confident, energetic, highly intelligent dogs – which makes them great family pets. Their name comes from the Latin *terra*, meaning 'earth', as Terriers were originally used to hunt small burrowing prey, such as rabbits, rats and mice.

MINIATURE SCHNAUZER

This neat little dog is a mix of a standard Schnauzer, Poodle and Affenpinscher.

AIREDALE

These brave little dogs were the first police dogs in the UK and worked with British soldiers in the First World War (1914-18).

JACK RUSSELL

This breed gets its name from the Reverend John Russell, who first bred them.

WORKING

A working dog is any breed that was traditionally bred to perform a job. This could include herding sheep, pulling a sledge, hunting large prey or rescuing people.

BORDER COLLIE

These sheep-herding dogs are said to be the most intelligent breed of dog.

HUSKY

These super strong dogs have a double coat of fur that keeps them warm in cold weather.

ST BERNARD

This iconic rescue dog is named after a dangerous spot in the Swiss Alps, called the Grand St Bernard Pass.

Pet **Expert**

DOGS

By Gemma Barder

PET EXPERT: DOGS!

Dogs are great! They are the world's most-popular pet and it's easy to see why. Dogs are loving and loyal, but they also need lots of care and attention. In this book you'll learn everything you need to know about looking after your dog, setting up the perfect home for them, and the best way to keep them happy and healthy. You'll also find out how dogs became such compatible companions, as well as some pretty incredible canine facts along the way. In fact, why don't we get started right away?

TOY

Toy dogs evolved from lapdog breeds (dogs that fitted nicely into the lap to be stroked and cuddled) as well as common breeds that have been bred to be smaller, such as the Miniature Poodle.

SHIH TZU

This famously adorable breed dates back at least 1,000 years and it comes from Tibet.

CHIHUAHUA

This pint-sized pup is the smallest dog breed in the world.

MALTESE

This well-mannered breed is thought to be the oldest European Toy dog breed.

THE OTHER DOG GROUPS INCLUDE:

GUNDOG: This group was trained to run to pick up any prey their owner had shot down. Golden Retriever, Cocker Spaniel, Poodle

PASTORAL: These dogs were bred to help look after, herd or guard livestock, such as chickens, pigs, cows and sheep. Bearded Collie, Corgi, Old English Sheepdog.

HOUND

Like Terriers, Hounds are hunting dogs. They have an incredible sense of smell, often long droopy ears, and they are strong and capable. This group also contains some of the oldest known breeds of dog still around today.

DACHSHUND

This breed's long, flexible body makes it perfect for wriggling into burrows after small animals!

WHIPPET

These friendly dogs are very quiet – so they might not make the best guard dogs! Some Whippets don't bark at all.

BASSET

Its floppy ears aren't just for show! They flap smells up from the ground, making this breed a super-sniffing tracker.

UNCOMMON DOGS

Dogs are everywhere, right? But there are actually some breeds of dog that are so rare, there are only a few hundred left. With powerful noses and tuneful barks, these dogs are pretty special.

OTTERHOUND

This breed comes from Britain and has a playful personality. Otterhounds were originally bred to hunt, but are now mainly show dogs and family pets. Despite their sweet nature, there are only 600 registered Otterhounds in the world.

Otterhounds are an ancient breed and have been around since the 1600s!

Otterhounds have webbed feet, making them great swimmers!

NEW GUINEA SINGING DOG

This musical little pup really lives up to its name. The New Guinea Singing Dog has a unique way of howling that is much more tuneful than other dogs. Although not many of these dogs live as pets, some people believe there could be lots more living in the wild.

TELOMIAN

These dogs were first bred in the Malaysian jungle, in Southeast Asia, and they are still the only breed of Malaysian dog that can be found outside the country. Telomians were originally kept to get rid of mice and rats (just like cats) but they are now mainly family pets. Although they don't look that different to other dogs, they developed brilliant climbing skills as their original jungle owners lived in houses on stilts!

FACT FILE

The most endangered breeds in the world are actually wild dogs.

■ The Ethiopian Wolf is found in the highlands of Ethiopia, Africa. Fewer than 400 are alive today.

■ The endangered Mexican Grey Wolf is half the size of its North American cousin. It is thought that there are only 114 left in the wild.

■ Darwin's Fox is actually a small wolf the same size as an average cat. It is endangered, with less than 1,000 in the wild.

TOP — **GOING DOWN**

In 2018, there were more French Bulldog puppies registered than any other breed in the UK, while the number of Welsh Corgis born continued to decline.

PUPPY PATTER

Dogs are great at communicating with their human buddies. Find out everything you need to know to understand what your puppy pal is trying to tell you!

FACT FILE

When you meet a new dog, there are a few things you should do to make a great first impression:

■ Ask the owner's permission before you say hello – some dogs can be shy or nervous.

■ Let the dog sniff your hand (sniffing in the doggy world is like shaking hands in the world of humans).

■ Speak softly and calmly to the dog.

TAIL

Dogs wag their tails when they are in a happy and playful mood. Your pup will usually wag its tail when it first sees you, or if you are playing together. Dogs put their tail between their legs when they are scared, sad, or even if they feel guilty about pinching food off the kitchen table!

BELLY

Your dog will show its belly when it wants to make friends with other dogs – or when it wants a tummy rub from you!

8

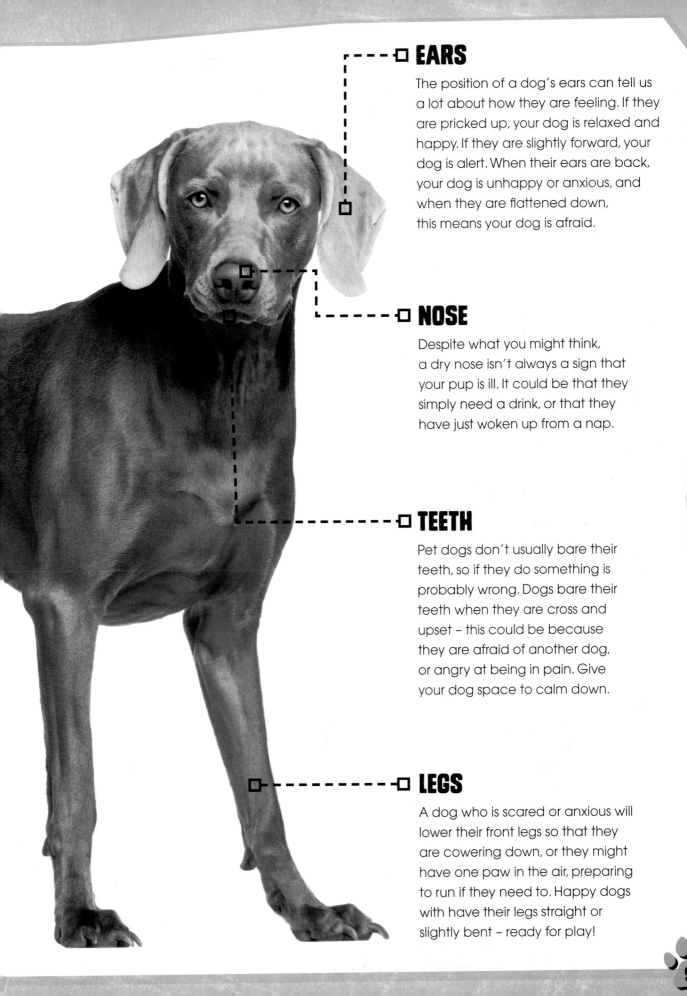

EARS

The position of a dog's ears can tell us a lot about how they are feeling. If they are pricked up, your dog is relaxed and happy. If they are slightly forward, your dog is alert. When their ears are back, your dog is unhappy or anxious, and when they are flattened down, this means your dog is afraid.

NOSE

Despite what you might think, a dry nose isn't always a sign that your pup is ill. It could be that they simply need a drink, or that they have just woken up from a nap.

TEETH

Pet dogs don't usually bare their teeth, so if they do something is probably wrong. Dogs bare their teeth when they are cross and upset – this could be because they are afraid of another dog, or angry at being in pain. Give your dog space to calm down.

LEGS

A dog who is scared or anxious will lower their front legs so that they are cowering down, or they might have one paw in the air, preparing to run if they need to. Happy dogs with have their legs straight or slightly bent – ready for play!

PUPPIES

These adorable little bundles need a lot of love and attention because they are no longer with their mother. Now, it's up to you to help them develop and grow!

PICKING A PUPPY

Picking the right puppy for your home is very important. Talk to your family about what type of dog would suit you best. Bigger dogs need more room and a big garden to play in, while long-haired breeds need plenty of brushing.

All puppies are cute when they are little, but they grow up fast!

BRINGING THEM HOME

Puppies can be quite nervous when they are taken to a new home. Make sure you have a comfy dog carrier to put them in and a warm blanket. If the journey home is long, make sure you have plenty of water and food for them, too.

Give your new puppy plenty of love and play with them every day to welcome them into your family.

FACT FILE

In the first few months:

- Find a vet and get your PUPPY used to visiting them.
- Train your PUPPY to wee and poo outside.
- Keep up to date with worming, flea treatments and immunisations.
- Ask your vet when your PUPPY will be ready to go outside. Then, take your PUPPY for short walks to get them used to other dogs.

DID YOU KNOW?

In some countries it is the law to have your new puppy microchipped. The tiny microchip placed painlessly inside your puppy's neck fold has all your contact information on it.

CARING FOR YOUR PUPPY

While your new puppy settles into your home, remember to keep things calm and quiet. They'll be learning all about their new environment – and all about you, too! Talk to a vet about what vaccinations your puppy needs to keep them healthy.

9 weeks

5-6 pups

Female dogs are pregnant for nine weeks.

An average litter has five to six puppies.

CANINE CARE

It goes without saying that you want your dog to be the happiest it can be. Find out the best ways to care for your dog.

NEW BEST FRIEND

Dogs are social animals. In the wild, they live in packs. Left on their own they can be quite unhappy, so spend plenty of time with your dog. You could play in the garden, give them a good brush or just tell them about your day!

KEEPING CLEAN

A happy dog is a well-groomed dog. Grooming means making sure your dog is brushed and clean. Different breeds will need different amounts of grooming, so make sure you know what's right for your pet.

WALKIES!

One of the most important parts of looking after a dog is exercise. Dogs need to be walked at least once a day and some breeds need more exercise than others. Make sure you have a good lead, some dog treats and a poop-scoop with you.

DID YOU KNOW?

Clipping a dog's nails is tricky and is best done by a vet. You can also take your dog to a grooming parlour (a doggy hairdresser) to get their fur and nails trimmed.

Dogs need two bowls: one for a constant supply of fresh water and another for their daily meals.

FLEAS AND WORMS

Although it's not very nice to think about, fleas and worms are a common problem for dogs. The best way to help your pet is to give them monthly treatments to stop them from picking up fleas and worms. Your vet will be able to tell you the best type of treatment for your dog.

2 months

3 weeks

Dogs need their claws trimming every two months. Don't bathe any dog more than once every three weeks as it could irritate their skin.

FACT FILE

TRAINING DAY!

It's a good idea to teach your dog the following basic commands:

SIT

This is important when waiting to cross the road on walks.

STAY

When you don't want them to follow you.

COME

Vital for getting your dog to come back to you when they are off the lead.

FETCH

A fun throw and retrieve game to keep your dog happy and fit.

Give your dog lots of fuss and a little treat when they do something right!

THE CANINE CODE

There are lots of rules to follow when you own a dog, and it can get quite confusing! Follow these simple guidelines to become the perfect dog owner.

DO:

introduce your dog to other dogs to get them used to being around other animals.

give your dog a short name – one or two syllables is best. And avoid names that sound like commands!

pick up your dog's poo using a biodegradable bag, put it in the bin and wash your hands afterwards.

give your dog plenty of toys to play with. They like to be kept active.

check your dog's paws after they've been on a long walk.

treat your dog like one of the family. Dogs love to be part of a pack!

DON'T:

**pull or tug a dog's tail.
It will hurt and confuse them.**

**leave their water bowl empty
or dirty. Dogs need fresh
water to keep them healthy.**

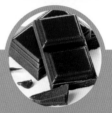

**force them to play with dogs
they aren't used to.**

**give your dog chocolate.
Chocolate is poisonous to dogs.**

**leave your dog alone for
long periods of time.**

**let them off their lead unless you
are in a large field or park
where this is allowed.**

✔ FOOD FOR DOGS ✘

 dry dog food	fish	chocolate	onions
wet dog food	apple	avocado	nuts
yoghurt	cheese	dried fruit	grapes

THE BEST BED

When you love your pet you want to give them the best home possible. Find out how to make a safe and cosy home for your dog.

SAFE AND SOUND

Making your house safe for a dog is a bit like baby-proofing. Look around the rooms your dog will call home to spot any dangers, such as wires they might chew on, blinds they could get tangled in or cleaning products they could mistake for treats or toys.

BEDTIME

A dog's bed is very important to them. It's not just the snuggle factor you need to think about, it's where you position their bed, too. Make sure your dog's bed is somewhere they can watch family life go by and feel as though they are part of the action.

THE GREAT OUTDOORS

Your pup should spend lots of time in the garden, so you will need to make it a fun and safe place to be. Check that there are no holes in the fence and that the garden gate is secure. Keep an eye out for any poo and clear it up straight away.

KEEP IT CLEAN

Keeping your dog's home clean and tidy is an important way to keep them healthy. Wash their bowls out once a day and wash their bedding once a week.

FACT FILE

Here are some dog beds to choose from:

NEST

A round, padded middle with soft edges that forms a cosy nest. Perfect for small to medium sized dogs.

CAVE

These beds have little hoods and are great for dogs that feel the cold, such as hairless breeds.

COT

Great for large dogs with lots of fur, they sit just off the ground so the fur doesn't get tangled.

MATTRESS

Looks just like a mattress for people! Perfect for large dogs who like to spread out.

DID YOU KNOW?

Dogs love toys! They help keep your dog occupied and relaxed, and stop them chewing other things, like the furniture!

WALKIES THROUGH TIME

Dogs have been our best friends for a very long time. Learn how our four-legged pals have travelled through history with us.

STATUS SYMBOL

As thousands of years passed, dogs became seen as symbols of wealth and power. Ancient Egyptian pharaohs, Chinese emperors and Roman nobility all had dogs as companions. Romans used dogs for hunting, and the strongest breeds were sent back to Italy to breed there, too.

38,000 BCE

3100 BCE

1200s-1400s

WOLF HEART

The first domesticated canines are thought to be wolves who followed human tribes around, looking for scraps of food. Some believe this could have started as early as 40,000 years ago! Over time, wolves started travelling with tribes and humans began training them.

POSH PETS

Nearly all aristocracy and senior clergy had pet dogs, which is why dogs often pop up in portraits of important people. Noblewomen preferred smaller dogs that they could rest on their laps, while noblemen liked powerful hunting dogs.

DID YOU KNOW?

In 1789, a Newfoundland dog saved a man from drowning in the sea off the coast of Portsmouth, UK. The man was so thankful, he bought the dog from his owner, named him Friend and created a coat of arms just for him!

The Basenji is one of the most ancient breeds of dog in the world. It is said to resemble the dogs kept by ancient Egyptian pharaohs.

A HELPING PAW

In the 1950s, a study done by a psychologist called Boris M Levinson (1907–1984) showed how dogs could be used in therapy sessions. He found that people were more relaxed and able to talk when a dog was around to make them feel safe and happy.

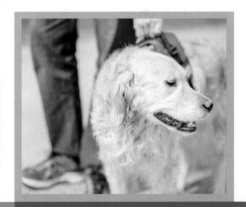

1870s

1950s

2000s

VICTORIAN LOVE

By the Victorian era, most middle-class homes had a dog. In 1873, The Kennel Club began registering the breeding of pedigree dogs in the UK. Soon after, in 1881, the American Kennel Club was formed. Both hold dog shows, such as Crufts in the UK. Queen Victoria (1819–1901) entered six Pomeranians in the 1891 Crufts dog show.

DOGS TODAY

Dogs are still the most popular pet in the world (closely followed by cats!). They have continued to serve and help humans in many different ways, including rescuing people, herding cattle, guiding the blind, aiding the police and being loving companions, plus so much more!

DISTINGUISHED DOGS

Dogs have such great personalities, it's no wonder some become famous! Find out the fascinating stories behind some of the most well-known pooches.

TOTO

Toto is the scrappy little pup who joins Dorothy on her adventures in The Wizard of Oz. He has appeared in books, films and television series based on the world of Oz and has even had a book written from his perspective: Toto: The Dog-Gone Amazing Story of The Wizard of Oz.

LASSIE

Some say Lassie first appeared as a character in a short story by Elizabeth Gaskell. Others believe she was based on a real dog who saved a sailor's life in the First World War. However, Lassie became known all over the world thanks to the 1940s film Lassie Come Home and the TV shows that followed.

DID YOU KNOW?

The first dog to play Lassie was actually a boy called Pal! He played the part for 11 years.

CORGIS

Queen Elizabeth II (1926–) was first given a Welsh Corgi puppy on her 18th birthday and she went on to breed them for many years. Her last Corgi was called Willow and was the 14th generation of the queen's first ever pup. Queen Elizabeth has had more than 30 Corgis during her reign.

SCOOBY DOO!

Scooby is a Great Dane who helps his friends to solve spooky mysteries, as well as making time to eat Scooby snacks with his best friend, Shaggy. The first **Scooby Doo** cartoon was shown in 1969 and the dopey dog is still around today. There have been TV shows, films and even video games featuring Scooby and the gang.

$10,000 $125

Moose the dog was paid $10,000 per episode to star in the American TV series, *Frasier*. The little dog who played Toto in *The Wizard of Oz* was paid $125 a week (which was more than most actors got paid in 1939 when the film came out!).

TOP DOGS

Big, small, brave and… unusual! All these dogs have something in common – they are all record breakers!

TALL AND SHORT

Gibson, a Great Dane just like this one, measures a massive 107 cm tall, while Milly the teeny Chihuahua is just 9.65 cm which is about the same height as a mobile phone!

This little **Chihuahua** is still much bigger than Milly!

SPACE DOG

Laika was a very special dog. In 1957 she became the first animal to orbit Earth. What the space scientists learned from her trip helped make it possible for humans to travel safely in space.

9 million

69 million

There are about 9 million pet dogs in the UK.

There are about 69 million pet dogs in the US.

Australian **C**attle **D**ogs, like this one here, can live for a very long time!

OLDEST DOG

A hard-working Australian Cattle Dog named Bluey became the oldest ever dog in 1939, when he lived to 29.5 years. The average age of a dog is between 8–15 years, although some smaller breeds can live longer.

LONGEST TONGUE

Mochi the St Bernard is the lucky owner of the longest dog tongue in the world. It measures 18.58 cm and is so big it usually lolls out of his mouth. Despite his claim to fame, his owners think he is the cutest dog on the block.

Many St Bernards, like this one here, have long tongues!

DOGGY DATA

If you think you know everything about dogs, be prepared to be amazed. Memorise these five fab facts to impress your friends.

1 CANINE NOSES ARE UNIQUE

The print a dog's nose makes is one of a kind, just like human fingerprints.

2 TIRED PUPS HAVE PRIMAL INSTINCTS

Dogs curl up to sleep because of their wild dog past. Wolves curl up to keep warm and protect their vital organs.

3 DALMATIANS DON'T ALWAYS HAVE SPOTS

When Dalmatians are born they are almost always pure white. Their spots develop as they grow.

4 GREYHOUNDS ARE SUPER SPEEDY

They are the fastest breed of dog and can run at over 72 kilometres an hour.

5 LABRADORS ARE SO PUP-ULAR!

In fact, Labradors are the most registered breed of dog in the world. They make good pets for families with lots of energy and space for them to grow.

YOUR DREAM DOG

Can we match your personality to your dream dog? Answer the questions and follow the flow to find out!

WEEKENDS ARE FOR ...?

Relaxing

DO YOU LOVE READING?

Yes

Sometimes

Activities

I'm a bit shy

DO YOU LIKE MAKING NEW FRIENDS?

I love it!

No

ARE YOU IN A SPORTS TEAM OR CLUB?

WHAT'S BETTER? SPOTS OR STRIPES?

Stripes

Spots

Yes

DO YOU LOVE LONG WALKS IN THE COUNTRYSIDE?

Yes

Sometimes

No

ARE PARTIES ALL ABOUT DANCING?

Yes

Drama

AT SCHOOL DO YOU PREFER PE OR DRAMA CLASS?

PE

Maybe

FANCY A RUN?

OK

TIBETAN TERRIER

Sit down, relax, take a deep breath. That's your guide to life! You're a super chilled-out person who loves long walks as much as curling up by the fire with a good book.

CHIHUAHUA

Ooh, look! A group of people! There must be something fun going on over there! Just like Chihuahuas, you love being part of the action and making new friends.

DALMATIAN

If you can sit down long enough to read this you'll realise that you and Dalmatians just love being active and having fun. You're also naturally super stylish. Spots are so in!

QUIZ!

Now let's put everything you have learnt in this book to the test! Yes, it's time to find out if you truly are a doggy expert.

1 WHERE DOES THE NAME 'TERRIER' COMES FROM?

a) the name of the person who started breeding them

b) the Latin name for 'earth' because Terriers like digging

c) the word 'terror' because they can be quite fierce

2 WHAT SHOULD YOU DO WHEN YOU SEE A DOG YOU DON'T KNOW?

a) ask the owner if you can stroke it

b) run over and stroke its back

c) throw it a ball

3 HOW LONG ARE DOGS PREGNANT FOR?

a) one month

b) nine weeks

c) six months

4 HOW OFTEN SHOULD YOU WALK YOUR DOG?

a) at least once a day

b) once a week

c) once every two weeks

5 WHICH OF THESE CAN BE POISONOUS TO DOGS?

a) chicken

b) rice

c) chocolate

The answers can be found on page 30.

6
WHAT TYPE OF BED IS PERFECT FOR HAIRLESS DOGS?

a) cave
b) mattress
c) cot

7
WHAT TYPE OF DOG DID QUEEN VICTORIA ENTER INTO CRUFTS?

a) Welsh Corgi
b) Labrador
c) Pomeranian

8
WHAT STORY FEATURES TOTO THE DOG?

a) Cinderella
b) The Wizard of Oz
c) Mary Poppins

9
WHAT DOES A DALMATIAN'S COAT LOOK LIKE WHEN IT'S BORN?

a) white
b) spotty
c) hairless

10
WHICH OF THESE IS NOT A NEW BREED OF DOG?

a) Otterhound
b) Labradoodle
c) Cockerpoo

GLOSSARY

BREED
A group of dogs who share a specific set of characteristics

CANINE
A Latin word that means 'dog', or anything relating to dogs

CARRIER
A plastic container big enough to transport your dog in. It's usually made out of plastic with lots of air holes and a handle for carrying smaller dogs.

DOMESTICATED
Animals that are living with humans as pets or working animals

ENDANGERED
At risk of extinction

GROOMING
Looking after your dog's appearance. This can include brushing, bathing and nail clipping.

HOUND
A hunting breed of dog

HUNT
To track down animals to capture or kill. Lots of dogs were originally bred and kept to hunt pests on farms.

KENNEL CLUB
An Organisation in the UK that oversees lots of doggy events and practices. They also have a list of registered breeders.

PUPPY
A young dog. Dog's stop being puppies at various ages depending on their breed

TERRIER
A small dog that was traditionally used to hunt out animals by burrowing in the earth

TOY
The name for very small breeds of dog

VACCINATION
Injections for puppies to prevent them from catching nasty canine diseases

VET
An animal doctor

WORKING
A collection of different breeds who have all been traditionally used for work

WAG
The tail of a dog moving swiftly from side to side

QUIZ ANSWERS

1. B.   2. A.   3. B.   4. A.   5. C.   6. A.   7. C.   8. B.   9. A.   10. A.

INDEX

Published in paperback in Great Britain in 2020 by Wayland
Copyright © Hodder and Stoughton, 2019
All rights reserved
Editor: Dynamo Limited
Designer: Dynamo Limited
ISBN: 978 1 5263 0860 3

Printed and bound in China
Wayland, an imprint of
Hachette Children's Group
Part of Hodder and Stoughton
Carmelite House
50 Victoria Embankment
London EC4Y 0DZ
An Hachette UK Company
www.hachette.co.uk
www.hachettechildrens.co.uk

MIX
Paper from
responsible sources
FSC® C104740
FSC
www.fsc.org

Picture acknowledgements:

**All images courtesy of Getty Images iStock
apart from: P1 Shutterstock, P7 tr Shutterstock,
P7 Westend61 GmbH/Alamy 7 cr
(Key: tr-top right, cr-centre right)**

Every attempt has been made to clear
copyright. Should there be any inadvertent
omission please apply to the publisher
for rectification.

CONTENTS

YOUR PONY FROM HEAD TO TAIL

Ponies have sturdy bodies, strong bones, short legs and a rounded shape. They have tough hooves and grow a thick winter coat, so they can live outdoors all year.

Withers: The bony ridge between a pony's shoulder blades.

Tail: A pony uses its tail for balance, expressing itself, and swishing away insects. The area around the top is known as the dock.

Hock: The equivalent of a human's ankle.

Fetlock: The joint above the hoof.

Frog: The triangular part of the sole of the foot that touches the ground.

Pastern: This sloping part of the foot acts as a shock absorber.

PONIES

First published in Great Britain in 2019
by Wayland

Copyright © Hodder and Stoughton, 2019

Editor: Victoria Brooker
Produced for Wayland by Dynamo
Written by Pat Jacobs

FSC
www.fsc.org

MIX
Paper from
responsible sources
FSC® C104740

HBK ISBN: 978 1 5263 1005 7
PBK ISBN: 978 1 5263 1006 4

10 9 8 7 6 5 4 3 2 1

Wayland, an imprint of
Hachette Children's Group
Part of Hodder and Stoughton
Carmelite House
50 Victoria Embankment
London EC4Y 0DZ

An Hachette UK Company
www.hachette.co.uk
www.hachettechildrens.co.uk

Printed and bound in China

Picture acknowledgements:

**All images courtesy of Getty Images iStock apart from: p6 Fell pony
Shutterstock, p16-17 tc Alamy, p18 tr Shutterstock, p24 tr Alamy**

(Key: tc-top centre, tr-top right)

Every attempt has been made to clear copyright.
Should there be any inadvertent omission,
please apply to the publisher for rectification.

The website addresses (URLs) included in this book were valid
at the time of going to press. However, it is possible that contents
or addresses may have changed since the publication of this book.
No responsibility for any such changes can be accepted by either
the author or the Publisher.

Ears: Ponies can swivel their ears and pick up sounds all around them. The sensitive area just behind the ears is the poll.

Mane: The coarse hair that grows from the crest helps a pony to swat away insects. The tuft at the front is called the forelock.

Crest: This is the top of the neck, underneath the mane.

Eyes: Because a pony's eyes are on either side of its head, it has a blind spot right infront and behind.

Muzzle: This is very sensitive. It includes the mouth, chin, lips and nose.

PONY FACTS

A pony is a small horse less than 14.2 hands tall at the highest point of the withers. A hand was originally the width of a man's hand, but it is now 10.16 cm (4 in). Ponies have stockier bodies than horses.

Cannon: The part of the leg between the hock and the fetlock.

TRADITIONAL PONY BREEDS

Ponies have adapted to live in cold, harsh environments. They have developed into tough and intelligent smaller-sized horses that are easy to keep, making them perfect family pets!

Dales ponies are known for their intelligence, stamina, strength and courage. Dales ponies are calm and kind. They have large, tough feet and strong legs with feathered fetlocks. They are sure-footed and good all-rounders.

Dartmoor ponies are reliable and hardy. They stand no more than 12.2 hands high and are usually bay, brown or black. Their size and kind temperament means they make excellent children's ponies, but they are strong enough to carry a small adult, too.

Fell ponies have heavily feathered legs and feet with strong hooves that don't often need shoes. These clever characters make good all-round family ponies, but they can be headstrong. They are sure-footed and especially suited to carriage driving.

Exmoor ponies are strong and stocky. They have adapted to cold weather and grow a waterproof winter coat with built-in insulation. These ponies are about 12 hands on average. They are good with children and adapt to all kinds of equestrian activities.

COAT COLOURS

Ponies' coats come in a variety of colours. Here are a few:

- **Bay** – rich brown body with black legs, mane and tail
- **Chestnut** – reddish-brown with no black points
- **Dun** – sandy coloured body with black legs, mane and tail
- **Roan** – an equal mix of white hairs and a pony's basic body colour, eg bay roan
- **Grey** – grey ponies have black skin with white, grey or black hair, and look grey or off-white. Pure white horses have pink skin and are very rare.

Welsh ponies are divided into sections A, B, C and D according to their size. Their personalities make them popular pets for children and they make good driving ponies, too. There's no upper height limit for section D, so many are classed as horses.

Connemara ponies are smart and willing. 'Connies' love to jump, but can turn their hooves to everything from carriage driving to dressage. These gentle, good-natured ponies are easy to keep, and at up to 14.2 hands, are great for child and adult riders.

Hackney ponies are medium-sized, high-stepping ponies. They have broad shoulders, a smooth back and a high tail. Easy to keep, they have loveable personalities. They are perfect for pulling carriages, but also make good riding ponies and companions.

Shetland ponies stand up to 10.2 hands high. They can survive harsh conditions and sparse grazing, and easily get overweight. These little ponies are intelligent and crafty – a bored Shetland will get into all kinds of mischief, so they need to be kept busy.

FIND YOUR PERFECT PONY

Buying a pony is exciting, but it's easy to fall in love with the wrong one, which can make riding less fun and unsafe. Like humans, ponies are individuals, so take time to find your perfect partner.

CHOOSE AN EXPERIENCED PONY

A young, inexperienced pony may be cheaper to buy, but it will take time to train and there's no guarantee it will be safe and reliable. It's best to choose one that is at least five years old and has been well trained so you can start riding it straight away. Ponies can be ridden into their twenties, so you will have many years of fun ahead!

SIZE IS IMPORTANT

When choosing a pony, the rider should be able to mount from the ground and their feet should not be much lower than the pony's belly. Ponies should not carry more than 20% of their bodyweight, including tack. It's tempting to buy a pony that's too large if you're still growing, but it may be difficult to control and it's a long way down if you fall.

TOP TIPS FOR PONY BUYERS

Ponies are expensive and the wrong one could be unsafe for you. Here are some tips to help.

• Take someone with you who has lots of experience with horses and ponies for independent advice.

• Choose a pony to match your skill and fitness. Your riding instructor may be able to advise on which sort of pony would suit you best.

• Handle the pony yourself and perform all the day-to-day activities, such as catching, leading, grooming and tacking up.

• Watch the pony's owner riding it before you try it out and then ask to spend some time alone with your potential new pal.

• Ask about the pony's history and look at its horse passport. If a pony has changed hands many times, it could point to a health or behavioural problem. Check that its vaccinations are up to date.

• If you are seriously interested in buying a pony, ask a vet to examine it. It can be difficult to get insurance without a pre-purchase veterinary report.

BUY  BORROW

You can borrow a pony from a private owner or a horse charity. The upkeep costs and responsibilities will be the same, but a pony on loan from a charity will be well trained and health checked. They will be able to offer you support and advice, too!

HEALTH CHECK ☑

• A pony should be inquisitive and alert.

• Its coat should be shiny and smooth.

• The eyes should be clear and bright.

• Its ears should be pricked, held forwards or to the side, or flicking backwards and forwards.

• The nose should be clean and the pony's breathing should be regular and steady.

• The pony should walk comfortably and evenly on all four feet.

A PLACE TO LIVE

You'll want to have everything ready to welcome your pony to its new home so the move is as easy as possible. If you've never cared for a pony before, sign up for a horse care course and take riding lessons if you're not a confident rider.

STABLING

Ponies grow thick, waterproof winter coats. Their gut produces heat as it digests fibrous food, so they have built-in central heating. They love being outdoors, but it's a good idea to put ponies in a stable at night or during bad weather. They also need to be inside if they're ill so it's easier to care for them. Stables must be well ventilated, but not draughty and make sure door bolts are pony-proof – some clever ponies learn how to open them!

PADDOCK PREPARATION

Paddock fencing must be built with horses in mind. Barbed wire is dangerous if your pony runs into the fence, and it could get its hooves caught in sheep mesh. Ponies need about 0.4 hectares (1 acre) of grazing each. Remove things that might harm your pony, such as wire, glass, bricks, stones, rubbish and poisonous plants. Fill up, or fence off, any holes. Ponies drink up to 40 litres (10 gal.) of water a day so you'll need a water tank specially designed for horses.

LIVERY

If you don't have room for a pony at home, you can keep it at a livery yard. Keeping a pony in livery will mean it has some horsey companions, and you can also get help and advice from the staff and other owners if you like. You may have access to a manege or indoor arena, too. There are different levels of livery depending on how much you are willing to pay and how much work you are prepared to do.

LIVERY CHECK

- DIY livery just includes grazing and use of a shelter or stable. The owner is responsible for all the pony's care.

- Part or assisted livery includes some help from the yard staff, such as feeding, turning out and mucking out.

- Full livery is expensive. It normally includes bedding and feed, and livery staff are responsible for all the pony's care including exercise.

- Working livery is sometimes offered by riding schools. The cost of keeping the pony is reduced because they use it for riding lessons.

UNDERSTAND YOUR PET

I'm a social creature and I don't like to live alone, so please make sure I have at least one pony pal.

BEDDING DOWN AND TACKING UP

Get some bedding to make your pony pal a soft, warm bed when it arrives. This is also the time to get all the equipment you'll need to ride and care for your new friend.

A COMFORTABLE BED

Ponies can sleep standing up, but they do like to lie down sometimes, so they need a soft bed to protect their joints. Choosing the best bedding for your stable will depend on your storage space and whether your pony is sensitive to dust, or has allergies.

Straw is cheap, but messy to store and takes up lots of space. Some ponies are allergic to it, while others like to eat it. It makes good garden compost, but it's bulky and soon makes a large muckheap.

Wood shavings are easy to store and ponies won't eat them. Droppings and wet shavings should be removed quickly to avoid a build-up of ammonia. Shavings take longer to rot down than straw and cheap brands contain lots of dust.

Shredded paper is useful for ponies that have allergies, but a large amount is needed to make a good bed. It gets blown around easily, which can make the area around the stable and muckheap untidy.

Wood pellets are eco-friendly, dust free and very absorbent. Wet patches are easy to spot and quick to remove, and it composts quickly. The pellets need soaking in water before use, which takes extra time.

Rubber matting is dust-free and easy to clean with a hose. It's expensive, but there are no extra costs. Extra bedding may be needed in a draughty stable. The stable needs good drainage and, without bedding, your pony may get dirty.

ESSENTIAL EQUIPMENT

You can save money by buying some equipment second-hand, but make sure everything is thoroughly disinfected before use. Second-hand saddles should be checked by a saddler to make sure they fit properly. Some sellers include a pony's saddle and tack so check whether you'll need to buy these. Here's a list of equipment you'll need before you bring your pony home.

EQUIPMENT CHECK ☑

- A well-fitting saddle and a saddle pad or numnah
- A bridle and bit
- A head collar
- A lead rope
- A grooming kit
- Feed and water buckets
- Mucking out equipment
- A first aid kit: bandages, cotton wool and antiseptic
- Fly repellent (if necessary)

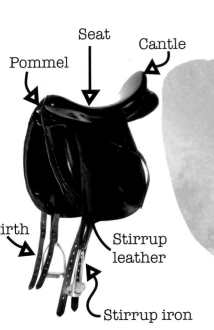

Pommel
Seat
Cantle
irth
Stirrup leather
Stirrup iron

UNDERSTAND YOUR PET

Bank up the straw at the edges of my stable, otherwise my legs may get stuck against the wall and I won't be able to get up again.

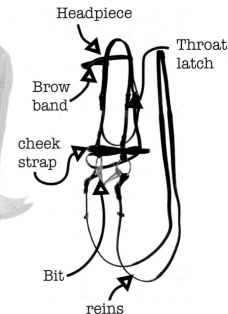

Headpiece
Throat latch
Brow band
cheek strap
Bit
reins

RIDING WEAR

A well-fitting riding hat protects you from serious injury. Make sure yours meets the current safety standards – it's best to buy from a shop with a professional hat fitter. Boots should have smooth soles and a small heel so your foot doesn't slip through the stirrups. They must be sturdy to protect your foot if a pony steps on it. Jodhpurs or riding breeches are more comfortable than jeans, for both you and your pony, and a high-visibility jacket is essential if you plan to ride on the road. Optional extras are gloves and a body protector in case you fall.

WELCOME HOME!

Moving to a new home can be very stressful for a pony. It has to get used to new companions, a different stable and paddock – and even the water may taste different! Try to find out as much as you can about your new friend's usual routine so you can introduce any changes slowly.

A NEW DIET

It's best to feed your pony the same food it's used to eating to start with. If possible, you should take some hay from its old home and gradually add your own to reduce the risk of colic. If you're turning your pony out, restrict it to a few hours' grazing at first and increase it slowly. Make sure it drinks enough. If not, it may not like the taste of the water so try adding a little sugar or molasses.

QUARANTINING A NEW ARRIVAL

If you have other horses or ponies, let them see the new pony from a distance at first. It's important to keep them separated for at least two weeks to avoid spreading diseases or infections. Use different food and water buckets, mucking out and grooming equipment, too. If you're caring for several horses or ponies, change your overalls and disinfect your boots when you move between them for the first few weeks. When the time comes to introduce your pony to others, turn it out with just one companion at first.

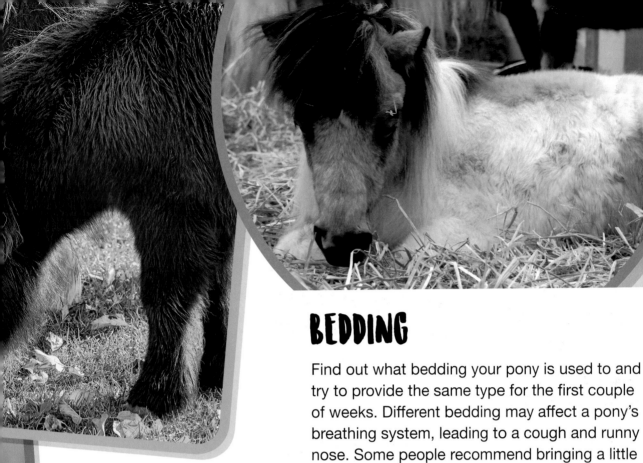

BEDDING

Find out what bedding your pony is used to and try to provide the same type for the first couple of weeks. Different bedding may affect a pony's breathing system, leading to a cough and runny nose. Some people recommend bringing a little of your pony's old bedding to its new home, so it smells familiar.

HEALTH CHECKS

Register your new pony with a vet and a farrier as soon as possible in case a problem arises. Try to avoid the stress of dental treatment, vaccinations, worming and shoeing while it gets used to its new home. It's normal for a pony's behaviour to change after moving, but if it shows signs of a cough, high temperature or loss of appetite, call your vet immediately. Once your pony has settled in, get it checked for worms.

UNDERSTAND YOUR PET

Grooming is a good way to make friends with me.

FEEDING YOUR NEW FRIEND

Ponies need to eat little and often, so it's better to give them four small meals than two large ones. They can be greedy creatures, and eating too much rich food may cause serious health problems.

WEIGHT WATCHING

A pony's natural food is grass. In the wild ponies put on weight during the summer when grass is plentiful, and lose it over winter when food is scarce. The food we give ponies today is much richer than the rough grass they would naturally eat, and because they are often stabled or rugged over winter, they don't burn off the extra fat. If your pony is overweight, give it less food over winter and don't use a rug so it burns energy to stay warm.

THE BEST DIET

Ponies have small stomachs and a very long digestive system that breaks down tough plants. They need bulky food like grass to keep their food moving through their intestines, or it can get stuck and cause colic. While grass and hay should be the main part of the diet, if a pony is exercised regularly it will need small amounts of concentrated feeds, such as cereal or sugar beet. A pony's gut is full of friendly bacteria that break down plant foods, so always change its feed gradually to give its digestive system a chance to adapt.

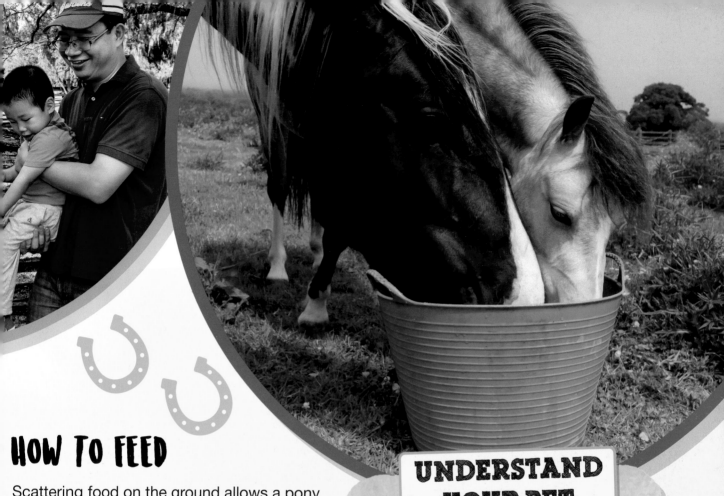

HOW TO FEED

Scattering food on the ground allows a pony to eat in a natural way, but it's wasteful and earth may be picked up with the feed, so it's best to put concentrated feeds in a bucket. Hay can be left in a pile on the ground and, although there will be some waste, this is safer than using a haynet because ponies can get their feet or necks caught in the net.

POISONOUS PLANTS

Some common plants can be very dangerous for ponies. Learn to recognise them and remove them, or fence them off. They include ragwort, rhododendron, foxglove, yew, privet, laurel, bracken, buttercups (harmless in hay), lily of the valley, deadly nightshade, laburnum, St John's wort, sycamore and oak (leaves and acorns).

UNDERSTAND YOUR PET

I love treats such as carrots and apples, but cut them lengthwise and take the cores out of apples, otherwise they may get stuck in my throat.

EVERYDAY CARE

Caring for a pony is hard work and you'll probably spend more time mucking out and grooming than riding. Are you up for the challenge?

PONY CARE

Daily tasks:

- Mucking out
- Grooming
- Exercising
- Feeding
- Topping up water troughs
- Picking out hooves
- Checking for signs of illness or injury

Weekly tasks:

- Removing droppings from pasture
- Checking paddocks for hazards
- Scrubbing out food and water containers

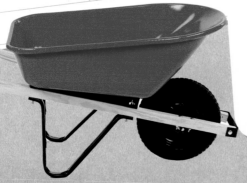

PONY CARE CALENDAR

Here's a list of jobs that are essential to keep your pony fit and healthy – and they have to be done whatever the weather! Your pony will also need regular visits from the farrier and vet for hoof trimming, reshoeing, worming, dental care and immunisations.

MUCKING OUT

Stables need cleaning at least once a day. You'll need a fork, rubber gloves, a shovel, a broom and a wheelbarrow for this job. Move droppings and wet bedding into the barrow, then sweep the floor and leave it to air for as long as possible. Then you can replace it with the clean bedding and top it up. If you can't turn the pony out, move it to one side of the stable and clean half at a time. Keep your tools away from its feet!

FOOT CARE

You should check your pony's feet every day and remove any dirt or stones using a hoof pick. Always work towards the toe so you don't damage the frog or the pony's leg if the pick slips. Ponies that are worked on roads or hard ground may need shoes to protect their hooves. Hooves should be trimmed by a farrier every ten weeks for unshod ponies, and every six weeks for shod ponies.

GROOMING

Grooming keeps your pony's coat and skin clean and healthy. It also strengthens the bond between you, and it's a chance to check for injuries. Use a curry comb in small circular movements in the opposite direction to the hair growth to loosen dirt. Flick away the dirt and loose hair with the dandy brush, then use a soft body brush to remove anything left on the surface of the coat. Clean your pony's face with a sponge or cloth and use a separate sponge or cloth for the dock area. Never share brushes and cloths between ponies because this can spread infections. Finally, untangle the tail and mane with your fingers, then brush or comb them.

YOU WILL NEED:

- A plastic or rubber curry comb
- A dandy brush
- A soft body brush
- Two damp sponges or soft cloths
- A mane comb or brush

UNDERSTAND YOUR PET

Sometimes when you're grooming me you might touch a very sensitive area and I may kick, so stand at my side, and never behind my back legs.

PONY BEHAVIOUR

Ponies communicate with one another using body language. By giving signals to other members of the herd, they are able to establish their position within the group without fighting.

YOU ARE THE BOSS

Wild ponies live in herds ruled by a stallion and an alpha mare who decide the position of all the other group members. Pet ponies also need a leader and, as ponies are large, strong animals, it's important that the leader should be their owner.

PUSHY PONIES

Ponies that are challenging your authority will crowd and push you, walk in front when you're leading them, and nip, bite or kick and step on your foot. The best way to show a pony that you're the boss is by earning its respect, which means you should be kind, but firm. Ponies can sense fear, hesitation and anger so always act calmly and confidently, and if a pony tries to move into your space, push it back.

UNDERSTAND YOUR PET

If you come straight towards me, looking me in the eye, I will probably run in the opposite direction because this means 'go away' in pony language.

EXPRESSIVE EARS

Ponies have very sensitive hearing and their ears are a clue to what they are thinking:

- Ears pricked and facing forward mean a pony is happy and interested in something.
- Ears lowered to the sides normally mean a pony is relaxed.
- Flicking ears show that a pony is listening and paying attention.
- Ears pinned flat against the neck are a warning sign that the pony is annoyed or unhappy and you should beware.

TAKING FLIGHT

Ponies are always on the look out for predators and are ready to flee if something frightens them. They have sharp senses of smell and hearing, so if they suddenly react they may have heard a noise you didn't. Pricked ears, wide eyes, flared nostrils and a raised head are a warning that a pony may bolt. If you're a nervous rider, your pony may sense this and be more jumpy. You could take lessons to gain confidence.

PONY HEALTH PROBLEMS

Ponies don't make a fuss when they're in pain, so you need to be aware of any changes that might mean they're unwell. Get to know your pony's normal heart rate, temperature and breathing rate so you'll spot if something is wrong.

LAMINITIS

Laminitis is a painful condition that affects ponies' hooves. It starts with slight lameness and can get so bad that the bone of the foot sinks through the sole and the pony has to be put to sleep. It can be caused by a past injury, stress, infection, or being worked for too long on a hard surface. Being overweight or a diet with too much sugar can cause it, too. To avoid this, be sure not to overfeed your pony and restrict grazing on sweet, new spring grass. Treatment should be given as soon as possible, so contact your vet immediately if your pony shows signs of lameness.

COLIC

Colic means stomach pain and it's common among ponies. Wild ponies graze on low-energy food throughout the day. Pet ponies often have just two feeds of rich food a day, and their guts haven't adapted to the change. Other causes can be dental problems, worms, stress or a change of diet. Signs of colic include rolling, lying down for long periods, looking at or kicking the stomach, curling the upper lip, sweating and restlessness. Call the vet if you think your pony may have colic.

STRANGLES

Strangles is a common infection of the nose and throat that is easily spread. A pony with strangles will have a high temperature, loss of appetite, yellow pus draining from the nose and abscesses may appear on the sides of the throat and head. Ponies can recover after a few weeks with good nursing.

WORMING

Ponies swallow worm eggs or larvae while they graze which develop into worms in the gut. Worms lay millions of eggs that end up in the pony's droppings ready to be swallowed by another pony. Ponies get large and small redworms, roundworms, pinworms, threadworms, tapeworms, lungworms and bots. Worms are becoming resistant to wormer medicines, so have droppings tested to check the number of eggs before giving medication. Removing droppings from paddocks regularly helps reduce the eggs your pony eats.

TOOTH TROUBLE

A pony that has bad breath, drops half-chewed food, drools, eats slowly or loses weight, may have tooth trouble! Make sure your pony has regular dental checks so any problems can be treated before they become serious.

Pony manure infected with round worms.

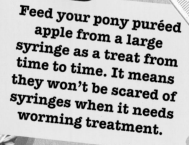

Feed your pony puréed apple from a large syringe as a treat from time to time. It means they won't be scared of syringes when it needs worming treatment.

TRAINING

Your pony needs to learn good ground manners before you start riding it. This may take time and patience, but riding a pony that doesn't respect you is very dangerous.

GROUND MANNERS

A pony with good ground manners will stay out of your personal space, stand patiently, and allow you to clean its feet and groom it. It will also accept being haltered and led, and let you put on a bridle and saddle without moving. If a pony bites, kicks or rears, it's not safe to ride.

EARN THEIR TRUST

Wild ponies trust their leaders and follow whatever they do, so to gain your pony's respect you need to show that you're a confident leader. Ask for help from an experienced horse or pony keeper. Once your pony recognises you're the boss, don't let it get away with bad behaviour. Horses always challenge their leaders because positions in a herd change. Never train a pony by losing your temper or hurting it. Ponies are much stronger than people and it may fight back.

CATCHING YOUR PONY

Ponies can be hard to catch. If they're busy grazing, they don't always want to be interrupted. Try approaching your pony from the side and talking to it. Then offer it a treat or give it a scratch in its favourite place and walk away so it doesn't always associate being caught with something unpleasant. When you go out with a head collar, keep it hidden behind your back. Although you may be cross with your pony, you should never show this when you finally catch it.

LIFTING A FOOT

If your pony is well trained it should be used to lifting its feet for cleaning and trimming. It's best to have someone to hold the pony and keep it calm while you do this. Stand to one side and stroke its back or shoulder, so it knows you're there, then run your hand down the back of the leg. When you reach the fetlock joint, lean gently against the side of the pony and lift up the foot. Never stand where you could get kicked. Remember, ponies can kick forwards and backwards.

FUN AND GAMES

One of the main reasons for getting a pony is to work as a team and have fun together! Taking part in games is good for bonding and it stops your pony getting bored.

GYMKHANA GAMES

Here are some games you can play alone with your pony, or you can get together with friends to compete against each other. Set up your arena first and make sure you have room to turn safely.

Pole bending race – Set up five poles (or cones) in a straight line about 7 metres (23 ft) apart. The pony and rider should weave through the poles to the end of the line, then turn around and come back. The fastest time wins, but there's a five-second penalty for missing out, or touching, a pole.

Potato race – Two potatoes are placed on a barrel at the far end of the course and riders have to gallop to pick up one potato at a time then place them in a bucket back at the starting line. The winner is the rider who gets both potatoes in the bucket in the quickest time.

MAKE A PONY TOY

Rinse out a large plastic milk container and cut some holes in the side that are just a little larger than your pony's treats. Put some treats into the container and screw the lid back on. Your pony will have lots of fun playing with the container and trying to get the treats to fall out.

MAKE YOUR OWN PONY TREATS

These homemade treats are packed with all your pony's favourite foods. You can experiment with your own ingredients, but never give your pony chocolate, maple syrup, rhubarb or milk.

Ingredients:
1 grated apple (pips removed)
2 grated carrots
80 g (1/4 cup) molasses
2 tablespoons vegetable oil
125 g (1 cup) whole-wheat flour
85 g (1 cup) rolled oats
1 teaspoon salt

Preheat the oven to 180°C (350°F, gas mark 4).

Mix the apple, carrots, molasses and oil together in a large bowl, then add the flour, oats and salt. Mix together and roll into small balls. Line a baking sheet with non-stick baking paper and bake the treats for about 20 minutes until they are golden brown.

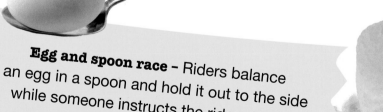

Egg and spoon race – Riders balance an egg in a spoon and hold it out to the side while someone instructs the riders to trot, canter, gallop and perform different manoeuvres. The last rider with the egg still in their spoon wins.

UNDERSTAND YOUR PET

I need to be kept busy, otherwise I'll make my own fun – and my owners don't always like that!

PONY QUIZ

By now you should know lots of things about ponies.

Test your knowledge by answering these questions:

1 **What are a pony's withers?**

   a. The area around the tail

   b. The bony ridge between a pony's shoulder blades

   c. The joint above the hoof

2 **Where would you find a pony's frog?**

   a. On its foot

   b. On its back

   c. On its head

3 **What is the maximum size for a pony?**

   a. 12.6 hands

   b. 15 hands

   c. 14.2 hands

4 **What is special about a Shetland pony?**

   a. It is very small

   b. It has pink skin

   c. It is not very intelligent

5 **Which plant is poisonous for ponies?**

   a. Ragwort

   b. Foxglove

   c. Both of these

6 What does it mean if a pony's ears are pinned flat against its neck?

a. It is annoyed
b. It is relaxed
c. It is happy

10 What may be wrong if your pony rolls around kicking its stomach?

a. It may have worms
b. It may have strangles
c. It may have colic

7 Which body part is affected if a pony gets laminitis?

a. Tail
b. Hooves
c. Stomach

8 How often should you check your pony's feet?

a. Once a week
b. When it starts limping
c. Every day

9 Where should you stand to groom your pony or clean its feet?

a. At its side
b. Behind it
c. In front of it

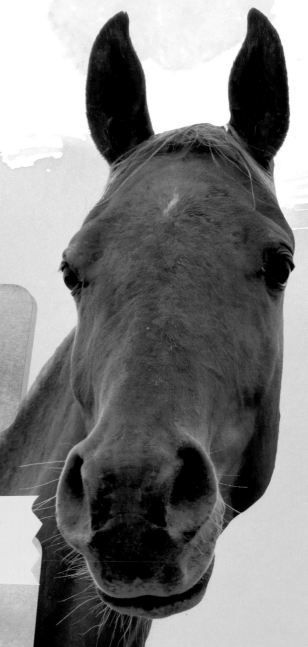

QUIZ ANSWERS

1 What are a pony's withers?

b. The bony ridge between a pony's shoulder blades

2 Where would you find a pony's frog?

a. On its foot

3 What is the maximum size for a pony?

c. 14.2 hands

4 What is special about a Shetland pony?

a. It is very small

5 Which plant is poisonous for ponies?

c. Both of these

6 What does it mean if a pony's ears are pinned flat against its neck?

a. It is annoyed

7 Which body part is affected if a pony gets laminitis?

b. Hooves

8 How often should you check your pony's feet?

c. Every day

9 Where should you stand to groom your pony or clean its feet?

a. At its side

10 What may be wrong if your pony rolls around kicking its stomach?

c. It may have colic

GLOSSARY

abscess – A painful swelling on the skin, filled with pus, usually caused by an infection.

alpha – The leading animal in a group.

ammonia – A strong-smelling gas that is produced when urine reacts with bacteria in bedding or on the stable floor.

bacteria – Microscopic living things that are found everywhere. Some are dangerous and cause diseases, while others are helpful and keep animals healthy.

bit – The part of the bridle that sits in a pony's mouth.

bridle – The straps and metal fittings that are placed over a pony's head to control it.

curry comb – A tool with short teeth: plastic or rubber curry combs are used to bring dirt to the surface of a pony's coat; metal curry combs are for cleaning brushes.

dandy brush – A hard bristled-brush that should be used carefully, and only on ponies with very thick coats.

dressage – Training a pony to perform a series of movements.

equestrian – Connected with horse riding.

farrier – Someone who trims and shoes horses' hooves.

feathered – Long hair on the lower legs of some pony breeds.

fibrous food – Food that has to be chewed, such as grass and hay.

head collar – Straps that fit behind a pony's ears and around its muzzle so it can be led on a rope.

headstrong – A pony that likes to get its own way.

horse passport – A booklet that shows a pony's age, markings and breed, and lists all its owners.

immunisation – Injections that protect a pony from disease.

lameness – Limping or having trouble walking normally.

larvae – Young or newly hatched worms or insects

livery – A stable where staff look after other people's horses.

manege – An enclosed area for training horses and riders.

mare – A female horse or pony.

mucking out – removing dirty bedding from a stable.

numnah – A saddle-shaped pad, which is placed under the saddle.

pus – A thick yellow or green liquid that forms in infected flesh.

rear – To stand up on the back legs with the front legs off the ground.

saddle pad – A square or oval pad that cushions the saddle and absorbs sweat.

stallion – An adult male horse or pony.

tack – Equipment used to ride or lead a pony, such as saddles, bridles, head collars and lead ropes.

turning out – Putting a pony outside to graze.

worming – Giving a pony medicine to kill any worms or eggs in its digestive system.

INDEX